M000248870

When Loving Him Is Killing You

Journey to Wholeness

Goldia Felder

BluSoul Worldwide Publishing

ISBN 978-0-9829031-1-7
When Loving Him Is Killing You: Journey to Wholeness

Copyright © 2011 Goldia Felder
Published by- BluSoul Worldwide © 2011

The author makes no apology for how the very **REAL** presence of God in this work of non-fiction may impact the reader's spiritual life. For ordering, booking, permission, or questions, contact the author.

Printed in the United States of America
First Printing 2011

Edited by: Shantae A. Charles for GOD Ideas, LLC
Cover Design: Chuckie Scott, Warrior Design
Cover Consulting: Robert O. Charles, ROC Studios International, Inc.

When Loving Him Is Killing You

Journey to Wholeness

Goldia Felder

BluSoul Worldwide Publishing

Dedication

This book is dedicated to my daughters and every woman who is dealing with the stress of life situations. It is because of my experience and my desire to see every woman live a happier and healthier life that I felt compelled to write this book. My hope is that it will give some insight and hopefully motivate you to let go of unhealthy situations. It's all about you.

Acknowledgments

Big thanks are due to God who has more wisdom than we could ever imagine or think to have. It is because of Him that I have survived so many setbacks in my life. He has truly brought me through the fire. So many facets of my life have become refined because of my trials.

To my Mother who has been my "Shero" raising six girls and five boys; I'm sure it was an eventful life experience. You are my angel divine and I love you. To my children Lisa, JP, Amanda and Jason; you light up my life. I could not have asked for better children. To Tori- even before you became my beautiful daughter in law, the things we shared made completing this book just that much more important. Also, big ups to Alfreda and Sherry; thanks for being tough on me at times and loving me through it all. Love to all my sisters and brothers. There is nothing like the love of family. To my cousin Daryl Middlebrook and my very good friend Marion Boyd (Mac B), thank you for having my back. When I kept losing information because of computer crashes and writers block, you wouldn't allow me to give up. You encouraged me to persevere.

To my manager Martha Edwards and MJ, who doesn't know it, but when I felt like giving up, many times you guys made things so much easier by showing genuine concern.

To my girls, Leslie Fabian and Shonda Hart, thanks for being hard on me when I needed it most. To Vandra (VV), Pam Sheffield, Shelia Kirby-Gray and Karry Moore; you guys are absolutely crazy but that's what makes me love you. What can I say except that if it wasn't for you guys really being in my life I don't know what would have happened. Thanks for being there for me. Lastly, to Nicole Jones; keep it moving girl! You are woman of purpose and I'm watching you.

When Loving Him Is Killing You

Journey to Wholeness

Goldia Felder

BluSoul Worldwide Publishing

Contents for Wholeness

Introduction 8

What is Love? 9

Understanding Love 14

Living in Denial 17

Evaluating Relationships 26

Damaging Impacts 36

Body Talk 41

Getting Your Life Back 45

Letting Go to Move Forward 52

Our Time Will Come 55

Red Flags 58

Real Women, Real Talk 61

When I Know Better...I Love Me 64

Real Love 68

Journey to Wholeness Journal 71

Introduction

So many of us have dreamed of that fairytale relationship where we meet our knight in shining armor. We date; we fall in love, get married and live happily ever after. But what do you do when it doesn't quite turn out that way? What do you do when those hopes and dreams are shattered? When happily ever after appears to remain just an illusory dream or worse, turn into a nightmare? What do you do when the person you trusted with your heart somehow becomes the one you have to protect your heart from, what then?

Many women have experienced this dilemma at some point and time in their lives. Some of you, who are reading this, are presently dealing with this issue. Some have been able to rebound while others have not. Some find themselves completely numb and paralyzed in the situation, and don't know what to do. There are others that know what to do but feel they are not strong enough. Also, there are other women who know what to do but in order to make the transition they need to know where to start. Instead of reaching out, they became secluded and depressed. Over and over in their minds they wonder what they could have done to have a different outcome. They are broken and feel a sense of hopelessness and despair.

Though this book may not give you all the answers, it is my hope that it will give you a starting point. Hopefully you will gain some knowledge as to how to start living a better life. You will understand that to continuously stress over situations and not get any type of relief is not okay. Your quality of life as it relates to your overall health is partly contingent on how you handle relationships. When it comes to love and relationships, we have got to ask ourselves the questions we try so hard to avoid. Sometimes we don't want to ask ourselves questions for fear we already know what the answers are.

But if you want to live a better life, if you want to live a longer life, if you want to be here for your children, to fulfill your purpose in life, then you've got to face the realties of the relationship you're in. You've got to ask yourself the hard questions. Ultimately, you will have to ask yourself the hardest question of all: "What do you do, when loving him is killing you"?

What Is Love?

Love has been described as a profoundly tender, passionate affection for another person. Love is a feeling of warm personal attachment. It has also been described as deep affection as for a parent, child, or friend. We all learn about love in many different ways. Our perception of love and its characteristics has been shaped and developed through our various experiences.

Even as early as infancy we learned to manipulate and control our external surroundings. With a faint whimper or boisterous cry, we recognized that this would bring someone into our little worlds. We could manipulate and get our Moms or Dads to do what we wanted them to do. Because of this emotion we can become deeply attached and dependent on others. So if there were a wet diaper, or a bruised elbow or an empty stomach, we knew someone would come to our rescue and we would be nurtured and taken care of by someone that "loved" us.

> Our perception of love and its characteristics has been shaped and developed through our various experiences.

When you first experienced love, you perhaps didn't quite understand exactly what it was that you were feeling. All you knew was that you felt these butterflies you felt in the pit of your stomach. Maybe you experienced sweaty palms or, a burst of anxiety. Maybe it was a combination of these feelings. What you did understand though, was that it made you feel warm inside. It somehow made us feel protected and gave us the wherewithal to face life with an attitude of strength and resilience. As a little girl, I remember experiencing all those feelings as early as elementary school. Now I know many of you are probably saying, "How could that be? You were too young to understand what love was." Yes, and hypothetically speaking, you would be correct. But remember when I said earlier how love makes you feel? While I may have been too young, I certainly remember feel this emotion inside that made me smile. This being said, indulge me for a moment.

One day my elementary teacher needed to leave the classroom for a few minutes. Now, each time she left, she would appoint a class monitor. This person would be responsible for reporting the names of any students who were disruptive, out of their seats, talking or did anything else that would be grounds for disciplinary action. On one particular occasion, the boy that was left in charge just happened to be the boy that made me feel those butterflies in my stomach. Now of course I wanted to be on my best behavior. Why do you think I wanted to be on my "best behavior"? When you love someone, you want to make them happy. You don't want to hurt them in any way.

My first goal in this instance was to get him to notice me. Once that part was accomplished, my behavior had to be on point. To get him to notice me through my behavior, i.e. not being disruptive by talking, getting out of my seat, etc, was my main objective. This was my strategy to get him to like me. If I was successful in all these areas, this presented the opportunity to get him to like me the way I liked him. I told you to humor me because that is just how my mind worked at that age.

> Sometimes there are no limits or lengths to which we will not go to in order to fend off feelings of rejection by someone we love.

While the other children were playing, out of their seats and being disruptive, I laid my head on my desk. I was as quiet as a mouse. Then it happened: "Why don't ya'll be like her and put your head on your desks?" I smiled. My heart raced in my little chest and I felt like I was on top of the world. *He had noticed me*, I thought to myself. *It worked!* I think I smiled the rest of the day. The best part of it all was that he did begin to like me. Many times we take these ideals into our adult lives. We do things to get others' love and attention. We try to win their affection by the things we say or do. Whatever we think will please them, make them happy or "love" us we have done or still do. Sometimes there are no limits or lengths to which we will not go to in order to fend off feelings of rejection by someone we love. Maybe you thought if you were loving, kind and giving, then he would somehow show you the same in kind.

Think of someone you've loved or even love right now. Think of some of the things you did to get their attention. Maybe it was a compliment. Do you remember as a child writing a love note? If you love me, check this box, if you don't check this box? Yes I'm sure most of us have written that one. Once you got his attention, to what extent did you go to in order to win him over or to have him in your life? Once he was there, to what extent did you go in order to show your love and affection for him? Maybe you went out and bought a gift for his birthday, Christmas or Valentine's Day. Maybe you wrote a special poem just for him. Maybe you "put your head on your desk" At any rate your goal was to show your love by the things you not only said but by the things you did.

A young lady I know well went as far as writing lyrics to some music. After completing the words she took the time and added them to the music on a CD. Now, I'm not absolutely sure but I think it took her about a week to complete. Afterwards, she presented it to the guy she was dating. How sweet was that? But her objective was complete. Sometimes we go above and beyond to show someone we love just how important they are to us. If you were one of those fortunate ones, you had the privilege of being raised in a nurturing home. Perhaps you had the opportunity to witness displays of affection by your parents. Maybe you received hugs and kisses on the cheek and were told how beautiful, smart and loved you were. There is nothing like an approval from someone you love.

On the other hand, there are those who were raised in homes just the opposite. They witnessed outburst of anger and tears. Some witnessed physical, emotional and verbal abuse and were at times the receiver of this same behavior themselves. Being predisposed to this behavior, your understanding of love became distorted and confused. Some struggled inside as they got older confused as to what was acceptable and what were not acceptable behaviors of love. Some rejected the lie that love behaved so badly, while others embraced it. Because of this many women find themselves accepting behaviors from their husbands or lovers that are none to be desired.

We find ourselves trying to hold on to that love by doing things, saying things, buying things, or anything else to not feel the rejection of that person we are in love with. Our value system and our self-esteem are chiseled away bit by bit until we are shells of women we once were struggling to find ourselves again. Trying to recover but not really knowing sometimes if we *ever* will.

I remember as a little girl playing with dolls, that there was always some kind of drama. There were fighting episodes, and crying episodes, cussing episodes and making up ones. She wouldn't want to get out of bed and would just lie there, crying. He would buy flowers, say I'm sorry; I will never do it again. He would say I'll do better and they would make up. They would be happy again for a while, until the next round. Sound familiar? Love had become synonymous to unhappiness, pain and depression. It was complicated and hard to understand.

> Our value system and our self-esteem are chiseled away bit by bit until we are shells of the women we once were, struggling to find ourselves again.

Many of the things we experienced growing up has distorted and deceived us into thinking things will get better. We think if we hold out, they will stop physically attacking us. They will stop drinking excessively. They will come home or call when they said they would call. We think, they will do what is needed to be done as the father of our children. That in time things will be like we have dreamed them to be. I will admit that I myself became extremely passive after seeing the passivity of my family members. Even in the midst of emotional, physical and sometimes violent behavior, they stayed. What should have been rejected behavior became acceptable and so the cycle began.

Many of us have experienced incest, rape, and other abusive behaviors. Some have been from one foster home or relative's home to another. In these experiences and others we try to conform in order to be loved and accepted because after all, who wants to be rejected? It's amazing how we can be programmed, conditioned and trained to do or not to do certain things all in the name of love.   Many women don't realize they deserve better than to be abused. They don't know anything else except to be used as someone's punching bag. It doesn't matter that they are emotionally, psychologically or physically abused, they have become accustomed to bad behaviors for the sake of what they think is love or worst yet out of fear of being alone.

We begin to accept those behaviors as normal because we are afraid and don't want those warm feelings that love initially brought us to end. We want to feel protected. We want that love to come running when we cry or we don't feel well. We want that love to be there when we are hungry and want to be filled with the joy that loving that person brings to us. We don't want to feel those negative feelings that accompany rejection. So, we hold on, and in some cases it kills us, either physically, emotionally, or spiritually. We cut short our abundant life for the hope of temporary affection.

> You are a part of the fabric of womanhood, and what you do, what you allow affects us all. You have to come to a point in your life that you began to give yourself permission to say "no!"

My fellow sisters, you need to understand how important you are. I want you to understand you matter if to no one else but to yourself. You are a part of the fabric of womanhood, and what you do, what you allow affects us all. You have to come to a point in your life that you began to give yourself permission to say "NO!" No, I will not be mistreated. No, I will not be used. No, I will not be abused. I deserve better! Give yourself permission to say no to behaviors that you have somehow come to accept as normal. When you begin to do this you will discover you are stronger than what you thought you were. You will begin to realize, you don't have to settle for being treated second class. You are" Class". Trust me. You will begin to live a much healthier and happier life.

UNDERSTANDING LOVE

Whether you want to be in a relationship, are in a relationship or have dreams of getting married or are already married, it is important to understand the dynamics of love. It is my belief that in order for a relationship to be successful it should encompass the four elements of love: Agape love, Phileo love, Storge Love and Eros love. Let's look at these aspects of love a little closer.

Agape

The greatest love that you can possess is Agape, or unconditional love. When all other love goes south, this love will be there. Agape love is only accessed through God. It is selfless, self-sacrificing love, and goes against human nature to fend for one's self. From a Biblical perspective, this Godly love is not based on the superficial such as what type of job a person has, what kind of car a person drives or the type of home a person owns. This love is not based on the premise that if an individual upsets us or disappoints us, that we will no longer love them. This is a love that goes beyond human frailty and faults. It goes beyond what is physical. It doesn't matter if one leg is longer than the other or if one breast is large or small. It doesn't matter if the hair is long, short or balding. It doesn't care if the person has curves or is as straight as a pole. This loves gives and expects nothing in return. It is selfless and seeks the welfare of the other person. It is what it is, unconditional love. There is nothing human about Agape. It is completely divine.

Phileo

Phileo love is most aptly termed as a tender affection for someone. A lot of friendships have the foundation of this love. As you spend time with a person, you begin to see qualities in that person that you like. You find that you are drawn to those characteristics. You can identify with them. You may be a person that loves comedy and find that this person has a great sense of humor. it feels great when you can love someone unconditionally as well as enjoy a tender emotional connection. It is a love that exhibits camaraderie and brotherhood.

Storge

Storge is familial love. This show of affection is innocent in intent and connected through the bonds of kinship. A show of affection can come in the form of a hug, a kiss or holding of your hand in times of crisis or triumph. We as women tend to need this type of love more so than men. That could possibly be because of the way we are socialized. Therefore, it is important that a man understands this facet of a woman. More importantly, women need to understand that it's okay to reciprocate this same love.

Eros

Eros love is part of the recipe for the making of a successful relationship. This love encompasses the physically intimate part of a relationship. It's only natural as human beings to at some point want to engage in sexual intimacy with the person we are experiencing all these facets of love for. Healthy relationships do not always lead to Eros, but all healthy relationships should be founded on agape.

This is most times the ultimate display of the love and affection we have for another person and it is best expressed in a covenant relationship. It is the merging of what I would like to call "two souls". It's very important that we really be mindful of this love. When we become physical with someone and all the other elements of love are present, this can form what has been coined as a "soul tie" and can become very difficult to overcome in the event the relationship does not work o

This is why I feel it is so important that before you engage in this type of intimacy with someone that you thoroughly understand the ramifications. When two souls connect and things go awry, it can become one of the most difficult parts of letting go in a bad relationship.

When those two souls disconnect, they each take with them the essence of the other person. This is why divorce can be so painful. It is not only the rending of a physical contract but a spiritual bond. This is why crimes of passion are committed throughout the world. Severing a relationship rooted in Eros can feel as though a part of your soul has been taken from you. Many cannot cope with this and require extensive counseling to heal from wounds that cannot be seen with the human eye. It is possible for one if not both parties to not possess these types of love. However, if all four types of love are present in a relationship it can be successful. There is nothing more satisfying than loving someone and having them loving you with all of these ingredients of unconditional, tender, affectionate and physical love.

Living in Denial
A Personal Experience

After being married very young, I didn't have the opportunity to truly experience dating. I was married for a number of years but soon the marriage ended in divorce. For the first time I found myself living the single life. For the first time as an adult I was somehow learning things I probably should have learned a long time ago. The ways that I had fantasized love should behave had somehow become lost in the ashes of a marriage gone wrong.

I was meeting people, going out on dates and just having a blast. It was exciting, it was fun and adventurous. Everyday brought about a new experience and profound lessons in the game of love. As I'm sure some of you can attest, at some point the dating scene got old. I found myself once again, wanting to settle down. I wanted someone steady in my life. Dating took on a different direction. I began to date with the intentions of finding someone who was ready to settle down and hopefully get married.

It was always easy for me to meet and strikes up a conversation with those who I thought were really nice guys. My friends would introduce me to them and I would introduce myself to some as well. After a couple of disappointing encounters I decided I would take a break from the dating scene and focus on finishing up my college degree.

A few months into my sabbatical, I was approached by a very handsome man. He stood about 6" 2' with brown baby smooth skin and a boyish smile. His eyes had an almost marble like appearance that hinted at a bit of mystery. As he passed by me, he smiled and spoke. His voice was pleasant and he appeared to be a pretty nice guy. We introduced ourselves and talked briefly. As our conversation came to a close, he asked for my phone number. I will admit I was tempted to give it to him. However, I had made a commitment to myself not to date for a while. I had come up with this excuse to give to anyone that would ask me out or ask me for my number:

"I'm flattered, but no. If it's meant we will meet again"

Kind of good line, I thought. I watched as he walked away in his cute work uniform looking a bit disappointed. Who knew that two years later I would meet this man again?

After my dating hiatus, I had gotten back into the dating scene and was once again hoping to run into "Mr. Right". Walking out of an office supply store, I was approached by a guy who looked very familiar. We introduced ourselves and before the conversation was over, we realized we had met before, two years before to be exact. We talked and this time, unlike the last encounter, we exchanged numbers. We began to date and it was wonderful! I had been out of a relationship for several months and was trying to be cautious. I had become relationship shy and was unsure about allowing myself to get too serious about anyone.

> When you've been through broken relationships sometimes you become guarded. You don't want to continue to make the same mistakes repeatedly.

 We continued to date and I began to feel more and more like he could be "The One." We began to spend more and more time together. I began to warm up to the idea that maybe *this* guy was one of the good ones. Although we spent time together consistently, I continued to be very guarded. When you've been through broken relationships sometimes you become guarded. You don't want to continue to make the same mistakes repeatedly. You certainly don't want to have to revisit those feelings of loss you felt after a breakup, especially if you were in love. My barriers and hesitance began to cause a strain on the relationship. I thought to myself that once we got over the initial transitioning period that new relationships often go through, we would be okay. After dating for a few months, I began to slowly drop my guards. We were doing well, or so I thought. I was happier than I had been in a very long time. I thought to myself, this is it.

While emailing each other back and forth one day, I asked The Question:

"When are we getting married?"

Although The Question was asked in jest, I didn't expect in a million years the response that was to follow. "We need some time apart," he said. I was shocked and didn't know what to say. My heart seemed to plummet. I felt off balance and confused. I certainly didn't see that brick coming or I would have ducked. The thing is I thought he was just kidding. I found out later, he wasn't kidding at all.

Sometimes as we are going along, we think everything is okay in our relationship and then it happens. Caught off guard we sit scratching our head and wondering what just happened. *Was it something I did or said? Did I move to fast or too slow?* We might even rehash the event and replay it over in our minds analyzing every detail. We call on our friend Ms. Denial and we try to carry on as though nothing has been said. But the sad reality is that the framework of our relationship has been shattered and may be irreparable.

> A relationship ceases to be a relationship without communication.

I consoled myself by saying it was just temporary. It was just a phase and everything would be okay. I was lulled into a false sense of security. We still spent time together and called each other. We still told each other, "I love you." But soon the times together became less and less frequent. The phone calls were consistent for a while and soon began to become few and far between. I would become more and more anxious about what was going on. After all, a relationship ceases to be a relationship without communication. I now realize that I suffered from a serious case of denial. I was ignoring the signs. Although we were still saying those three words, even though he was still telling me it was temporary, I had closed my eyes and refused to allow my heart to see the truth.

His words were no longer matching his actions. We had begun to only see each other behind closed doors. The times we spoke on the phone were calculated. Whenever I called, no matter what time of day or night, he couldn't be reached. When we talked, he gave me the reasons why he wasn't able to answer his phone. I made myself believe his excuses whether it made sense or not.

He continued to drop by on occasions, but something was different. At times he would call and say he was on his way over. The next time I would hear from him there was and excuse as to why he never showed or even called. He often told me he still loved me and the things he would say to woo me gave me hope. It made me disregard the facts that were staring me in the face. I had closed my eyes to all the signs that were telling me something just wasn't right.

A short time later, while waiting on my vehicle to be detailed at a local shop, I began to talk to a young lady that was sitting nearby. We shared some very interesting information. We both had started getting strange phone calls. The phone calls had turned into text messages and emails from people we didn't know. They would introduce themselves as the girl friends or fiancés. Apparently they knew of us, but we had no idea who they were. It escalated to the point that I began receive harassing phone calls at work. I even received pictures of the man I believed to be The One on vacation with someone else.

In an effort to get to the bottom of the e-mails, phone calls and text messages, I decided I would question him. What better person to ask, right? I asked if he was seeing someone. I never could seem to get direct answers. I guess being the kind of person that needed a direct, precise answer didn't help. Needless to say, that was not what I got.

Unfortunately many of us are blinded by the love we have for people. Many times the answer is standing toe to toe, face to face and we refuse to admit to ourselves, the obvious. They are telling us everyday by their actions, yet we refuse to hear. Maya Angelou said that if someone shows you who they are, you should believe them the first time. I concur.

What was being said to me and what was being done was contradicting. The truth was obvious, but I was in love. Like so many women, I wanted to believe that the man I was in love with would never lie to me or withhold the truth.

> Unfortunately many of us are blinded by the love we have for people. Many times the answer is standing toe to toe, face to face and we refuse to admit to ourselves, the obvious. They are telling us every day by their actions, yet we refuse to hear.

Under what I would call normal circumstances, some women would have cut ties. Common sense would have kicked in or "kicked us" and said, "You need to move on and let that go." Unfortunately it may but we refuse to accept the naked truth about a situation. So many of us press forward and like a soldier we stare the lies in the face, it could potentially be detrimental, yet still we make the choice to let our hearts overrule our head.

How often have we closed our eyes to what we knew to be the truth? Maybe he didn't call for days and when he did he had an excuse. Maybe he said he had to work late, only for you to find out he was on vacation. Maybe he did something and proclaimed his undying love for you and said he would never do it again. He bought you flowers, or candy, or an extravagant trinket. Maybe he even started coming home at a decent hour. Perhaps he started wooing you the way he once did. But as soon as things seem to be going smoothly again, he begins to repeat the same patterns of behavior once more. Your gut instinct paired with reality is just knocking at the door of your heart.

Life's Guard, that inner voice, that thing we know as intuition is blowing a whistle and ringing bells. Red flags are waving and the sirens are going off in our heads but we turn a deaf ear because we don't want to face what we know in our hearts to be the truth: all is not as it seems.

Those feelings become more and more intense as time goes on. We continue to believe that things will change, that he will change. We even talk ourselves into believing that we could change him or at least change his mind. We try to secure the relationship with gifts, money or even sex.

Some women have gone so far as to think if they got pregnant they could salvage the relationship and that a child would make the man commit. They succumbed to Trap Him Syndrome. No matter what they did, he became more and more distant, more illusive. The more they did the worst things got. Now they find themselves not only alone but raising a child as a single parent.

No wonder we soon become nervous wrecks. We began to stress over what we can not change. Overwhelmed, we become preoccupied with the relationship to the point of obsession and depression. We become ill and now our body isn't healing as quickly as it once did. We're always feeling badly and we can't figure out what is going on.

We refused to face the truth of the condition of our relationships. But in order to stop living in denial, we must come to a point where we are willing to face the truth. We must be willing to accept the fact that the person we love does not love us the way we deserve to be loved.

What's really going on?

During my travels, sitting in the Nashville International Airport in Tennessee, I watched as passengers ran from one gate to the other. Some rushed with kids in their arms, while others looked back and forth confused as to which way they should go. Others just meandered around waiting for their next flight's departure. I sat by one of the windows to watch the planes taxi on and off the runway. As quickly as one landed there were several waiting to take off. I had been in Nashville visiting my daughter and was on my way back home. My flight would not be departing for another hour. I was hungry and decided to walk down to one of the nearby concession stands. I watched couples as they walked around holding hands, while others were making mad dashes to the departure gates. As I approached the stand, I noticed a couple standing in front of me. They seemed to be agitated. Now of course, in airports you expect that there would be some tension and anxiety, but this was different. It wasn't a look of frustration because a flight was missed. This look was more personal.

The woman stood with her arms folded and her back turned. Her eyes seemed glazed as if on the verge of tears. The gentleman at one point tried to talk to her but she just looked away not saying a word. He sighed and turned back towards the stand and placed his order. I couldn't help but wonder what had brought them to this point. What could have been said or done that was bringing her to tears. While in flight, I couldn't help but think about the couple at the concession stand. I began to think about my situation and how so often women have to deal with overwhelming circumstances in everyday life. Why is it that we settle over and over again to be in relationships that does not fulfill us or are not healthy?

While in flight, my daughter had left me a message. She had come across an article that she thought was interesting and wanted to share with me. I had been having difficulty going up and downstairs due to severe joint pain. Nothing I did or took seemed to work. This article she shared provided a number of reasons a person would experience illness that seemingly they were unable to get rid of and why. Some of the illnesses were allergies, immune deficiencies and with a certain emphasis that only your children can give, she stated that joint pain, had been linked to stress. I had shared some details of the circumstances surrounding the relationship issues I was having. I told her that I had ventured out more trips to the doctor in the span a few months than I had in an entire year. Even though the doctor had run test after test, she couldn't find anything wrong.

I would feel better for a while but whenever I would begin to think about my relationship issues, the symptoms would return. I was becoming increasing concerned because they would seem to be getting better, then start all over again and just added more stress. There were times my heart felt as if it would beat out of my chest. I would literally have to lie down and try to calm myself. Along with being the sole provider in my home, I now was starting to worry about my health issues. I would talk with friends and family members who would give me advice or some old remedy to take, but nothing worked. I didn't really know what to think or how to assess what was truly going on with me, my mind or my body.

Many of us are going around day after day, not having a clue why we are feeling anxious, or depressed, why we have no energy or appetite. We wonder why the crying spells, or why all we want to do is pull the covers over our heads and not face the next day. We feel better for a while but with no real lasting relief; so what's really going on?

> When we first meet someone we often represent or send out our best self when we are trying to make a good impression.

Think of a relationship that you possibly were in or are presently in. By evaluating the health of the relationship, you may be able to determine if it is causing you physical, mental, or emotional or other health problems. Most relationships begin with the persons involved being enamored with one another. I like to coin this as meeting each other's Ambassador. Ambassadors are high ranking officers that are sent to represent a government on a "temporary" mission. The ambassadors' job is to negotiate a treaty. They are given this authority by the person or the body of people that sent them.

What happens after the Ambassador leaves and the real person emerges?

When we first meet someone we often represent or send out our best self when we are trying to make a good impression. There may be an abundance of flowers, dinners, gifts or compliments. All of these acts heighten our emotional senses. We move into a state of blissfulness or what I would call the honeymoon stages of the relationship. But what happens when we begin to know things about each other that we didn't know before? What happens after the Ambassador leaves and the real person emerges? When we begin to know each other on a more intimate level, we begin to realize that sometimes the person isn't at all the person they presented themselves to be.

Evaluating Relationships

It is unrealistic to think that a relationship is going to be perfect or without error, seeing that there is that human factor in the equation. However, you should not allow yourself to remain in a relationship that is unhealthy. I don't think for one minute that we cannot determine when we are in an unhealthy relationship. While some things are not obvious, there is always that little voice within us that tells us something is wrong.

After doing some research and from my own experience, I have developed a few indicators that can help determine if your relationship is becoming toxic to your health. When viewing the indicators below, be true to yourself. It's so easy to try to paint a pretty picture of a relationship if you want it badly enough.

> While some things are not obvious, there is always that little voice within us that tells us something is wrong.

Are you are trying to hold on because you are afraid of what people will say? Is it because you parents were married for fifty years, and you want a marriage like your parents had? Or maybe your thought process was to be married and never divorce for any reason? Perhaps you met him during your high school years and he is all you've ever known. Some of you have children and want your children to have a home with both parents, which are ideal but can be destructive to the child's emotional well being if the relationship is abusive.

> It's so easy to try to paint a pretty picture of a relationship if you want it badly enough.

I can go on and on. Sometimes we feel we are so in love or we are so full of pride, that we allow those emotions to overrule what we know to be the truth. But allowing your pride or your heart or both to rule instead of being realistic about the situation you are in could prove to be detrimental or even fatal.

Identifying Healthy Relationships?

There are several ways you can determine if you are in a healthy relationship. I have provided some examples below. While not all may be present in any given relationship, some of them can be used as a compass to help you measure the health of your relationship. In being honest with yourself, you ultimately are the one that will benefit from honest answers.

Healthy relationships are when:

✓ **You mutually respect each other's opinions, ideas and feelings.**

While you are two different individuals, you have the ability to disagree on any given subject without being disrespectful. You feel that you have something of value to bring to the table. Whether it's the bills, the children, or where you're going on vacation, there is a mutual respect. It shows the maturity of both partners and can only strengthen the relationship.

✓ **You feel safe and secure with your partner.**

It's nothing like having the feeling that your partner is with you even when there are hard times. You know you have someone there that will make sure you are okay. If there is a threatening situation, you know your partner is going to step in and handle things if necessary. You know you can count on him when a situation arises with the children or with your car or with your home. No matter what, he's there for you. Your partner will not manipulate you or place you in unsafe situations or environments.

✓ **You are able to resolve your disagreements where both parties are okay with the decision.**

In relationships, there are compromises. It helps to know you have someone who will be willing to meet you half way. There are some things I feel you should never bring to the negotiating table such as, values, integrity or spirituality. When it comes to where you will live, if you should purchase a home or a car, or even what color to paint the room, you are able to talk about it together. Negotiating takes both people coming together not with the idea of winning but of compromise. You are able to come to an agreement that will work for all parties involved. This is a win-win relationship.

✓ **You both enjoy the time that you spend together, and have trust for each other when you are apart.**

How wonderful is it when you and your partner can spend time together making each other laugh or just hanging out? One of the things I find most enjoyable in a relationship is when you can sit quietly next to each other and you feel the warmth of their company. When you do silly things together or make your partner laugh without saying a word.

Even more important is the peace you feel in knowing that you can trust them. No matter what time of day or night you know that you can count on them being in the place they say they are going to be in. You have no fear because your partner has made you feel not only through words, but through actions that they are a trustworthy person.

✓ **Your partner supports you in the things that are important to you.**

Having the support of your partner when you have dreams and aspirations is exhilarating. To have someone on the side line rooting for you and letting you know you can do it, gives you the will to keep going when you feel you will fail. Whether its finishing college, becoming an artist, a singing career or aspiring to be a writer, whatever your goals are they are there. While you may be able to push yourself through self-motivation, it is so much better when you know your partner is there rooting for you. Two are better than one!

✓ **You know your partner respects your sexual boundaries.**

Today there are so many "anything goes" standards as it relates to the bedroom. However, when certain sexual activities are either against your religious beliefs or just a preference, your partner respects those boundaries. While we may all have our own individual idiosyncrasies neither partner will try to talk the other into doing something that makes them feel comfortable or violate their right to privacy.

✓ **You and your partner are honest and open with each other at all times.**

Honesty is a necessary part of any relationship. When both partners are honest and open with one another it contributes to and strengthens the feelings of friendship and intimacy. Always make it your business to be honest and open in your relationships. There will be times you may have thoughts to do differently. Sometimes the fear of what your partner will say, think or do may cause you to wonder or second guess if should be truthful. Most times your fear is only a perceived thought.

When you remain truthful, you never have to worry about telling a different story. The truth will remain the same today and tomorrow. Conversely, you will be able to look at yourself and know that your partner's heart can safely trust in you. If you can honestly say your relationship is on the right track after reading these indicators then hopefully your relationship is encouraging those around you who are in unhealthy relationships.

Identifying Unhealthy Relationships

Most of us know when we are in relationships that are not making us happy or healthy. The next set of identifiers should help you in determining if you are in an unhealthy relationship. Depending on your honest answers to these questions, you may need to determine if this is a relationship you should remain in. If you determine that it is not, for the sake of your present and future health you may need to rethink your current situation. Unhealthy relationships are when:

✓ He is controlling

In the beginning of a new relationship, it is not always easy to see the signs. Both people are putting their best foot forward in order to give the best impression possible. He may open the door for you, drape his coat around you when you're cold or even feed you from his plate. As you get comfortable with each other the real person becomes apparent. He may tell you he doesn't like your friends and wants you to stop hanging around them. He may even go as far as to keep you away from your family. These isolation tactics could become the prelude to more obvious mental or even physical abuses.

✓ You feel insecure.

I think that everyone deals with some measure of insecurity. But when it causes you to worry, suspect, investigate or question your partner's whereabouts, you may want to visit these feelings closer. Maybe it's because of past relationships. Perhaps he's cheated before and now you are questioning if he is able to be faithful.

Does he exhibit behaviors that make you feel uncomfortable? Does he make no effort to change those behaviors but instead he makes *you* feel guilty? If you are in a healthy, caring relationship with your partner there is no reason for you to feel insecure.

✓ **You need to know his every move.**

How many times have you sat at home or at work and wondered what your partner was up to? Did you become so engulfed with those thoughts that you couldn't function? How often do you find yourself calling just to see if he is where he said he would be? Or perhaps he still exhibits those same behaviors of infidelity that produces overwhelming anxiety.

While you may feel being in a relationship gives you the right to go through your partner's personal items, it does not! It is a definite sign of insecurity and distrust and a violation of their privacy. In a trusting relationship, you shouldn't feel the need to snoop through his pockets, take his phone to the other room to scan for unidentifiable numbers or confiscate his password to tap into his emails. This can only lead to more distrust between you and your partner.

✓ **You cry more than you smile**

Relationships are supposed to be fun and fill your life with joys. When you think about spending time with your significant other it should make you smile. How often do you find yourself crying over the relationship? How often do you find yourself sitting in your room asking "Why?" How often do you think about the broken promises and find yourself sitting alone in a corner wondering if he will keep the next promise? No relationship should have you crying more than you smile unless it's tears of joy.

✓ **You're depressed in the relationship**

Do you find yourself not wanting to get out of bed, or go to work? Do you find that the things you took pleasure in doing are not so pleasurable anymore? These are indicators that being in love should put a smile on your face and peace in your heart.

Ongoing depression can only cause your relationship to worsen. If you have become withdrawn, with no desire to participate in family functions that is a sign of depression. No relationship can survive when you or your partner is dealing with ongoing bouts of depression. You will struggle to help them maintain emotional stability while it takes an emotional toll on you.

✓ **You feel frustrated because you are not understood.**

You should always feel comfortable in expressing your feelings even if you don't agree on a particular topic. A feeling of frustration because you are not understood, is a clear sign that there is a communication problem. If there is no communication, there is no chance of relationship survival. You will only become more frustrated and withdrawn. You will find yourself saying what the use is. He doesn't listen; I'm just wasting my time.

✓ **Your partner does not support you.**

It is important that your partner supports your goals and dreams. Many times when there is no support, it could be a form of control. You may want to continue your education but he says no. You may want to start a business but he doesn't support that aspiration. It could be insecurity on his part and again will only lead to resentment in the long run.

✓ **Your partner always criticizes you or puts you down.**

Does your partner always critic everything you do? Does he put you down because of your weight, your education or lack thereof? Does he tell you you're unattractive or tell you, you need to be like someone else? This is unhealthy and behaviors like this over a period of time breaks down your self-esteem.

✓ **Your partner doesn't respect your feelings**

How often do you tell him his behavior upsets you? If staying out all night is a concern does he make light of it when you express your concerns? If you don't see him at least trying to correct the behavior then he really doesn't respect you or your feelings.

✓ **Your partner is physically or verbally abusive.**

According to the Bureau of Justice Statistics Special Report, U.S. Department of Justice 95% of women is the victim of domestic violence. Over 50% of women who are killed are murdered by their partner or someone that they know. At least 30% of physical disabilities in women are caused by domestic violence. Many of these abuses started out being only verbal. You should never have to live in fear of bodily harm to yourself or any of your family members. Absolutely no one deserves to be abused in any way.

✓ **Your partner uses drugs or abuses alcohol**.

Alcohol and drug addiction is a formula for disaster in any relationship. In relationships where alcohol is a factor, it is said that women are 3.6 times more likely to be abused by their partner. In the case of alcohol and drug abuse, it is estimated that 50% of all domestic violence which ends in death correlates with alcohol and/or drug uses at the time of the assault.

Many women are afraid to leave when they are in these types of relationships. There are however recourses to these situations. There are women's shelters available and by checking in your local area directory, you should be able to find the nearest shelter to you. You don't have to suffer in silence. Several states offer victim advocate programs as well that can assist with finding safe housing.

✓ **Your partner uses threats to control you.**

It is never okay for anyone to use threats of bodily harm against you or any member of your family. To do so violates the trust of any relationship. Whether they carry through with those threats or not, you can't take the chance that they never will.

Beyond threats of physical violence, your partner can also use other means of control. Some will use the threat of abandonment. This can be a very intimidating thing for a lot of women who do not work outside of the home or have more than one child. The loss of income or shelter finds many women struggling with leaving an abusive partner. They can also use the threat of self hurt, or other manipulating behaviors to make you feel guilty should you decide the relationship is not healthy or safe. Remember, you are not responsible for another person's behaviors or choices. Learn to recognize these behaviors and take the necessary steps to leave an abusive situation.

✓ **Your partner is overly possessive or jealous of your friends.**

Learn how to recognize the signs of jealousy and possessiveness. For instance, if after dating for a while you find your partner seems to get annoyed when you miss his phone calls. Or if he doesn't like you interacting with your friends or family members, these are clear signs of the need to control you. These behaviors are sometimes done out of jealousy and insecurities and are toxic to any relationship.

There are varying degrees, of indicators of unhealthy relationships. You have got to be willing to see them for what they are and make moves to do something about it. Displays of un-forgiveness, holding grudges, and bringing up past mistakes also point to a lack of trust in the relationship. All these behaviors can bring on undue stress. When you constantly have to deal with these unhealthy situations, you may begin to notice a decline in your overall health.

Damaging Impacts

Until I began to experience some of the medical problems I was having, I didn't know the toll it was taking and how stress could affect me in such a negative way. I began to research some of the symptoms in an effort to see how they were connected to stress, and the impact it was having on my health. I do recommend that you always seek professional medical help and not try to make your own personal diagnosis of your conditions. I share the following in an effort to open your eyes to the damaging effects of stress on your overall health.

Our Immune system

When dealing with ongoing stress, it's like being in a boxing ring. Our body takes a pounding. The immune system is weakened. When the immune system is negatively impacted our bodies become more susceptible to illnesses such as colds and minor infections. We can also develop major diseases. A person living with HIV for example may have an immune system further compromised by ongoing stress. A person with arthritis may experience frequent bouts with the disease and the symptoms may be more profound. Have you recently had a cold or other infection and it just seem to not get any better? Check your stress level. This could be a contributing factor why you're not getting any better.

Our Heart

Stress affects our cardiovascular system in several ways: When dealing with acute stress the heart works harder. Blood flow increases which can in turn increase blood pressure. You can experience an abnormal heart beat, and it may be harder for the blood to clot and the arteries can even experience some hardening. It is important to guard our heart from the issues of life that place unnecessary stress upon it.

Our Muscles

Stress can also manifest itself around the neck, shoulders and the lower back. This can cause headaches, backaches, and muscles spasms. For you or someone who deals with rheumatoid arthritis, continually stress can also worsen an otherwise mild condition. Stress can affect your ability to be active and mobile when you need to be.

Our Stomach

The stomach which is partly used in digesting food can now cause you to experience acid reflux, which usually manifests itself in the form of heartburn or acid regurgitation. You may experience constant hoarseness, clearing of the throat or persistent coughing. You may experience intestinal or digestive problems.

Our Lungs

Stress can worsen the symptoms of asthma. If you have asthma or other lung related problems, they can also worsen those systems as well. Our breathing can be shallow and rapid. Excessive yawning can also be a sign of anxiety which affects the breathing. Usually it is because we feel we are not getting enough oxygen in our lungs and feel the need to keep yawning in an effort to get more oxygen into our lungs and into our brain.

The Skin

Stress causes the formation of the stress hormones, adrenaline, cortisol and others. These hormones travel through our bodies taking with it side effects of increased sebaceous gland activity, reduced immune system response and increased inflammation. Our skin can manifest this activity in the form of breakouts, scaly skin or redness. Stress can make disorders such as acne or psoriasis worse.

When there is intense stress, it may trigger what is known as alopecia areata, a condition which stops the hair from growing. After a few weeks the hair falls out. Hair loss may start as a round patch and could possible spread throughout the scalp. It can also affect body hair. Although the hair may grow back, this process can start over again.

I came across an article by Jerome F. Kiffer, MA, and the Department of Health Psychology and Applied Psychophysiology. According to the article, stressful situations that continue without relief could lead to a condition called distress. Distress is a negative stress reaction. Distress can disturb our body's internal balance or equilibrium. This can lead to physical symptoms including headaches, upset stomach, and elevated blood pressure and worsen already existing medical problems.

Tension usually is one of the first sign of acute or ongoing stress. Our muscles tighten and feel hard when we touch them. When we are experiencing tension, we may feel excitable, irritated and unable to focus on tasks. Things that do not normally bother us, we seem to lose the ability to cope with them. We may experience upset stomachs, nausea or even diarrhea.

A few of the things I experienced were trouble sleeping, loss of appetite and my heart seemed to flutter in my chest sporadically. Sometimes I would just "check out." I tried to make myself numb to anything that was negative or I would sedate myself just to sleep. Other times instead of checking out, anything or anyone that appeared to be attacking me, I would fire back in the most vicious way I could without being physical.

For over a year I had been grieving the death of my relationship. For some reason I couldn't find a way to allow myself to move on. The relationship had flat lined for over a year and I was still trying to use my own defibrillators to bring the relationship back to life. This only proved to increase my anxiety and deepened the symptoms I was experiencing.

According to research 75% to 90% of all doctor's office visits are stress related ailments and complaints. Stress has been linked to at least six of the leading causes of deaths such as heart disease, cancer and lung ailments. It has also been linked to accidents, cirrhosis of the liver and even suicide. The lifetime prevalence of an emotional disturbance is more than 50% due to chronic untreated stress reactions. Half of the conditions of what we experience in our bodies can be attributed to unchecked or unresolved circumstances in our lives. We must take the initiative now to counteract the damage that has been done by stress.

Emotional Burn Out

In continually putting out energy to fix a relationship that only worsened over time, I began to realize how much my energy level had really dropped. When we continually beg our partner to stop drinking, to try to work things out, or spend quality time, we become more and more exhausted. The more we become fixated on "making it work" the more frustrated we become. We give and give of ourselves, our time and our patience until we become taxed beyond what we are able to continue to give. We become burned out. When we become burn out, we begin to lose our drive. We start to feel emotionally, mentally and physically exhausted. All we now want to do is, lie in bed or sit on the couch. We don't feel like eating or cooking dinner, or maybe we do just the opposite only to lower our self-esteem even more by too much weight gain. Things become less and less important until there is nothing left but an absence or suppression of our passion and drive.

Psychologist Herbert Freudenberger spoke of this condition in his 1974 book *Burnout: the High Cost of High Achievement*. Freudenberger said that burnout was the extinction of motivation or incentive, especially where one's devotion to a cause or relationship fails to produce the desired results. When we have gone above and beyond in trying to get someone to change without any positive results we over time become withdrawn. The things we once did to engage the relationship becomes less fizzles out until we begin to feel that nothing we do is working and therefore we cease trying to make the relationship work.

> It is time to pull the covers back, get out of bed and take your life back.

Burn out can cause negative emotions. It

can cause us to not be able to interact successfully with others. It can also cause us to perform below standards and can manifest itself in poor performance on the job or in educational pursuits. We underachieve even in the areas we once led or thrived in. Our minds continually wander back to the problems that we are facing in our relationship.

Many women are finding it difficult to put one foot in front of the other. No longer motivated, they wish only for the day to be over so they can once again return home, crawl in the bed and pull the covers over their heads. It is time to pull the covers back, get out of bed and take your life back. You must start today if there is to be a tomorrow.

Body Talk

One of the ways that you can take control of your life is to take control of your body. You've got one vessel that is intended to carry you through this life. Learn to listen and take notice of the signals that your body is trying to give you.

According to Nancy D. O'Reilly, Psych. D, Clinical Psychologist and founder of the Women Speak Project, our bodies react to stress in three different stages:

- **Alarm** - our body experiences perspiration, we have that sinking sensation in our stomachs, and our arms and legs begin to tighten

- **Resistance** —our body tries to repair itself but can't if the stress continues with no relief.

- **Exhaustion** – unchecked stress, ultimately leading to headaches backaches, insomnia and other health problems.

When our bodies go into "alarm" mode it gets ready for what is perceived as imminent danger or uncertainty. Our system does what I would like to coin as "get ready, get set" Remember when you were a child growing up? You undoubtedly played games where that phrase was used. Your heart raced inside your chest, you felt nervous and everything in you was hyped. Your body got itself ready to spring into action once they said "Go!"

In stressful situations our systems internal organs such as the heart, blood vessels, immune systems and sensory organs such as our brain and other's are modified to meet what is being perceived as danger. Some call it the "fight or flight" syndrome. Our brain sends signals that cause certain chemicals to be released such as steroid hormones (glucocorticoids) inclusive of the primary stress hormone cortisol. Cortisol regulates carbohydrate metabolism and the immune system and also maintains our blood pressure. The heart, lungs and circulatory system responds differently. Whenever the thing that is stressing us becomes more apparent, our breathing becomes more rapid and our lungs take in more oxygen. Blood flow may increase 300 to 400 percent preparing those organs along with the muscles for the job of dealing with the stress.

Another thing that stress does is shut down the digestive activity, a non-essential body function during short-term periods of physical exertion or crisis. In the case of continued or ongoing stress, this shutting down activity can cause dysfunction of the digestive system and cause constipation.

Stress related conditions that are most likely to produce negative physical effects encompass many factors, one of which is an unhappy relationship. Others of course are high stress jobs, family crisis persistent stress following a traumatic experience, and circumstances that we cannot easily control and the inability to inefficiently or insufficiently relax. Acute or ongoing stress can also adversely affect people with serious illnesses. Research suggests that there is a very strong connection between emotional health and heart health. Negative emotions such as anger, guilt and hostility can put you at high risk of coronary heart disease, stroke and even sudden death. Our body's attempt to repair the damage that has been caused by stress related incidences is referred to as resistance.

Although all stress is not considered bad, continual stress is. For our metabolism, the over activity of the ANS (autonomic nervous system) and increased cortisol secretion produce elevated levels of sugar in the blood or hyperglycemia. If prolonged, this can result in a rise of insulin. Insulin is the hormone produced by the pancreas to control sugar metabolism. If this situation continues for a long period of time, continued hyperactivity of the ANS and elevated cortisol will lead the body down the path to type II diabetes. Elevated levels of cortisol, as in depressive illness, are also linked to gradual demineralization of bone.

Dealing with acute or ongoing stress, the body becomes exhausted. Think about the times when you were dealing with stressful situations. There was no break or real down time that you experienced. You were unable to relax because it was always on your mind. The symptoms that your body produced under these conditions may have led to sleeplessness. Maybe you tossed and turned all night, or dosed off only to wake up suddenly only to discover you had been asleep for only 15 or 20 minutes. You experienced a loss of appetite or your appetite increased. For some you may have begun to experience headaches, backaches, joint pain or a combination of all of these. Although these are a few of the ailments that you can experience during acute stress, imagine how exhausted the body must feel over a period of time with constant bombardment.

Ongoing stress can also affect us psychologically. Studies have shown that the inability to adapt to stress is associated with the onset of depression or anxiety. Repeated release of stress hormones produces hyperactivity in the body. This causes a disruption of the normal levels of the nerve chemical called serotonin which is critical for the feelings of well being. Stress can lower the quality of life by limiting the feelings of pleasure and accomplishment.

Studies have shown that mental stress can be a major catalyst for angina. Angina is a condition that can manifest as a severe sore throat, in which spasmodic attacks of suffocating pain occur. Acute or ongoing stress has also been linked to a higher risk for serious cardiac problems. The heart can develop rhythm abnormalities and heart attacks. An emotional stress effect alters the heart rhythms and poses a risk for serious events or even death, thus dying from a broken heart becomes more than a cliché put a real possibility.

Many develop a loss of appetite. In some cases stress can trigger hyperactivity of the thyroid gland, stimulating the appetite but causing the body to burn up calories at a faster than normal rate. Muscular joint pain, headaches and even the inability to reach an orgasm has been linked to stress.

With so many health problems that women face daily on a regular basis, why continue to subject ourselves to stress over events that we have no control over? You can only control you.

After displaying almost all of these stress related symptoms. I realized there was more going on than I had imagined. I had weight loss, insomnia and depression. I was experiencing shortness of breath. I had acne breakouts, hair loss and my joint pain had worsened. Thinking it would help, I started taking pills, using all kinds of products on my skin and scalp to get some relief. When that didn't work I began taking pills to try to calm down my stress levels. Needless to say, those only prove to have short term results. I only consumed a couple of glasses of alcohol a week-- it now became more frequent.

I rationalized in my mind that a few drinks wouldn't hurt. I missed more and more days from work and my family suffered as well. The more I tried to resurrect the relationship I was in, the greater the anxiety and the worse the symptoms became. Depression was no longer a symptom but a lifestyle.

GETTING YOUR LIFE BACK

I finally got tired of waking up every morning feeling depressed and not wanting to get out of bed. I had grown weary of my heart racing inside my chest and feeling like I was going to just fall apart. I was tired of the aches and pains and the doctor's visits only to find nothing for the cause of my symptoms. I finally decided, no more.

I wanted to know how to get over my bouts with depression. I wanted to be healthy and whole again. I started reading books and researching. After discovering what was wrong and realizing that I couldn't do it alone, I sought professional help. Yes, I went to counseling. I knew I wasn't doing a very good job on my own. I wanted to feel better. I wanted to feel more energetic, healthy and happy again. With so many women facing this dilemma, I wanted to know how I as well as other women like me could survive and reclaim our life back. Many of us have had relationships like this. We didn't want to let go for whatever reasons. Maybe he was our high school sweetheart. Maybe you had been dating for a while and he was the father of your child or children. Perhaps you were married to him. Whatever your reason, you probably thought or felt your life would end. You no doubt are thinking just as I did, that if you could not resurrect the relationship you would stop breathing.

> As women, we need to know when it's time to let go. It's a fact of life that not everyone who comes into our lives is there to stay.

Well into the second year, I was still crying to my friends and family. I would hate the guy then love him. I would want to spend time with him and then try to make myself believe I wanted nothing to do with him. It was an emotional rollercoaster. He no longer wanted to be there and I was trying to make him stay. As women, we need to know when it's time to let go. It's a fact of life that not everyone who comes into our lives is there to stay. If you have been the best wife that you know to be, if you have been the best partner you can be and still they walk away, don't try to keep them there. If they still exhibit the behaviors that are unhealthy for you or you and your children, you need to let it go.

What's really important?

To try to keep someone in your life that doesn't want to be there or *shouldn't* be there will only add to your stress and anxiety. Trying to hold on to someone who obviously has no intentions of changing the behaviors that are affecting your health is detrimental. You need to find the strength to let it go. You will only grow to resent them.

One day an email was sent to me. I'm not sure of its origin. What I do know is it could not have come at a better time. The title of the writing was "Let It Go." I'd like to share of few of the excerpts from that writing.

There are people who can walk away from you. And hear me when I tell you this! When people can walk away from you: let them walk. I don't want you to try to talk another person into staying with you, loving you, calling you, caring about you, coming to see you, staying attached to you. I mean hang up the phone. When people can walk away from you let them walk. Your destiny is never tied to anybody that left. People leave you because they are not joined to you. And if they are not joined to you, you can't make them stay. Let them go.

And you've got to know when people's part in your story is over so that you don't keep trying to raise the dead. You've got to know when it's dead. You've got to know when it's over. Let me tell you something. I've got the gift of good-bye. It's the tenth spiritual gift, I believe in good-bye. It's not that I'm hateful, it's that I'm faithful, and I know whatever God means for me to have He'll give it to me. And if it takes too much sweat I don't need it. Stop begging people to stay. Let them go!! If you are holding on to something that doesn't belong to you and was never intended for your life, then you need to...LET IT GO! If you are holding on to past hurts and pains...LET IT GO! If someone can't treat you right, love you back, and see your worth...LET IT GO! If someone has angered you...LET IT GO! If you are holding on to some thoughts of evil and revenge...LET IT GO! If you are involved in a wrong relationship or addiction...LET IT GO! If you are struggling with the healing of a broken relationship...LET IT GO!

If you keep trying to help someone who won't even try to help themselves...LET IT GO! If you're feeling depressed and stressed ... LET IT GO!!! If there is a particular situation that you are so used to handling yourself and God is saying "take your hands off of it," then you need to ... LET IT GO!

If we will be honest with ourselves, we all have struggled with letting go of people who no longer wanted to be there. Whether it was family, friends or others, somehow we either felt or still feel the need to hold on. Many of us have our own individual reasons why we will not let go. We become stripped of our ethical rationalizations. No matter how unhealthy the relationship, no matter what it is doing to us psychologically, emotional or physically we can't seem to let go. It doesn't matter what excuse we use for staying in a bad relationship the excuses are fundamentally our way of rationalizing our reasons for staying.

> It doesn't matter what excuse we use for staying in a bad relationship the excuses are fundamentally our way of rationalizing our reasons for staying.

Many of us are so *devoted* to our relationship that we feel it is our "duty" to stick it out no matter how dysfunctional it may be. Some of us have been in a bad relationship so long that we have grown accustom to the bad behaviors. We idolize the relationship and camp out around what we perceive it to be while it destroys our spirit and bankrupts us, robbing us of all the hopefulness we entered into the relationship with.

We make the excuse that we have been together for so long that he's all we've known. Although the behavior negatively affects us, we adapt a method of numbness. We act "as if" what is being said or done is of no consequence. We make ourselves believe that we are use to it and become on some level accepting of the behavior. Yet somewhere in the back of our minds we are hoping that the situation will change or at the least, get better. We also become *fearful.* Many women stay in bad relationships because they feel they are financially unequipped to take care of themselves or if children are involved, their children. We fear the unknown more than the damage an unhealthy relationship is doing to us.

We wonder if leaving will in some way affect the children. Will they resent us for leaving their father? Will they in some way be psychologically scarred? We feel to leave the bad relationship is to be forever alone. Even the mere thought of them being with someone else frightens us. We would rather be in an abusive relationship, than to not be in one at all.

Then there are those of us who deal with low self-esteem. We think that if we let this one go, no one else will want us, that this is our last opportunity to find happiness or that our biological clock is running out. The worst part about this thought process is, the longer you stay, the lower your self-esteem becomes. To be subjected to physical, mental and verbal abuse constantly only corrodes your self-esteem even more. Instead of improving your appearance, you no longer take care of yourself. In letting your biological clock rule your decisions, you make an illogical or irresponsible choice for the father of your child.

> **Many women want to believe that a man is going to change his mind or behavior. We many times think that we are that magic potion that will make him do right.**

You don't want to hang out with your friends and begin to neglect your family members. You spiral into a state of depression. As the dynamics of relationships change, women are finding themselves leading lives of desperation. They are holding on to fears and beliefs about who they are and their self-worth. They are assuring themselves with the argument the fabricated idea that they will not be better off alone. Many women want to believe that a man is going to change his mind or change his behavior. We many times think, he just needs a good woman in his life that we are that magic potion that will make him do right.

We think if we stay around he will see the error of his ways and become this knight in shining armor. Some of us go even further. We play the game of "act as if". We act as if we don't care in hopes that he will think he's about to lose us. We think this will scare him into coming around and developing that "act right" gene. If it's not in him the behavior will only last for so long, then it's back to old habits.

When actors and actresses are on set, they are "acting" or "in character". They have their scripts and follow the instructions of the director. When the takes are over, when the lights, camera and action are gone, they are right back to being who they really are. Much like an actor, After all theatrical apologies are said in your relationship, he will be back to who he really is-- The apologies for hitting you, the "I will never do it again, I'll do better" scenes, the "I love you, kissing, hugging and sex scenes" may be for his benefit or the benefit of your family who knows something is incomplete. If there is no change, chances are you will repeat the scenes again and again. How many times will you allow yourself to play the role of mistress, sideline, sugar momma or punching bag? Only you can decide.

> How many times will you allow yourself to play the role of mistress, sideline, sugar momma, or punching bag?

I have known women who thought if they made more money, owned their own homes or rode in better cars that they could somehow keep a man from leaving. Trust me, if he doesn't want to stay, nothing you have, no gifts you purchase or the amount of sex you give will make him stay so let him go. We change things about ourselves and compromise who we are as an individual all for the sake of having someone in our lives. Women of all age groups are having more and more liposuctions, breast and butt implants and face lifts, life-altering procedures with known health risks done every day to please someone else. According to the American Society for Anesthetic Plastic Surgery, nearly 11.5 million cosmetic surgical and non-surgical procedures were performed in the United States in 2006 of which 92% were women. The number of procedures (surgical and non-surgical) performed on women was over 10.5 million, which was an increase of 1% from the previous year.

We need to begin to ask ourselves some very important questions. Questions such as why, and for whom are we making health altering decisions for? Am I doing this because I want to be loved? Do I think the person I'm in love with will love me more? But more importantly, ask yourself this question: *What do you do when loving Him is killing you?*

> **Why choose to hold onto a relationship you know is not healthy?**

What if you were told you had a malignant tumor and the only way for you to live was to have the tumor removed? Would you hold on to it for sentimental reasons or would you let them remove it so that you could live? *Exactly!* While that may be a bit extreme, unhealthy relationships could potentially have the same possible end. It would be ludicrous for you to try to hold on to something that you knew was going to eventually cost you your life if you didn't do something about it.

If something or in this case, someone is draining the very life out of you, you need to at some point decide when enough is enough and let it go. There are some things you can't change. There are some people in our lives that will never change no matter how much we want them to. Why choose to hold on to a relationship that you know is not healthy?

It doesn't matter what size dress or slacks you wear. It doesn't matter if your hair is black, blonde, short, long, natural or straight. Your eyes can be blue, hazel or green it is really of no true consequence. You have to come to a point where you understand these things don't really matter. What does matter is that you understand you have self-worth, and you are worth yourself. You are a full course meal, not just a side dish. You deserve to be The One and Only. If a man doesn't want to be with you, it doesn't mean necessarily that he is a bad person. It certainly doesn't mean that you are either. It just means that

> **You *deserve* to be The One and Only.**

you are two people that were possibly never meant to be.

Why waste time trying to beat a dead horse when you can be riding a live stallion? Don't waste your time crying over what could have been or how good you thought it was. If you find yourself being more depressed and unhappy about a situation, let it go. I don't care if he is the president of the largest corporation in the world or the unemployed man standing on the street corner, you deserve to be treated with dignity and respect. When it comes to your emotional, spiritual, mental and physical well being, there should be no compromise. No relationship that is affecting your health or wellbeing is ever worth it.

LETTING GO TO MOVE FORWARD

Breakups are never easy. Some days you feel like you are going to take your last breath. You cry and your chest feels tight. Somewhere in your heart you hope and pray that he will call. You don't dare get too far away from your phone for fear you'll miss his call. You feel even more anxiety when that call never comes.

Feelings of insomnia, anxiety or panic or heart palpitations may manifest. Nausea, headaches, agitation, excitability and confusion may bombard you. At some point you will go through an anger stage. You will think about the time and energy that you invested in making the relationship work. We inevitably will blame ourselves and question what we could have done better that would have caused the relationship to work. You will possibly go through a period of being numb. Some days you will feel like you can't put one foot before the other. It will be hard to get out of bed. You may wake up some mornings for work and find yourself picking up the phone to call in sick.

> You must give your former relationships a proper burial to fully embrace a new relationship.

I found that one of the mistakes we often make after a breakup is we try to stay attached in any way we possibly can. This only makes the loss and mourning period of the relationship and the transitioning period longer. To move towards healing you can't keep mementos of your Ex around. You have to get rid of anything that keeps them before you. If I had pictures, I either gave them back or put them away. If there were Birthday, Anniversary or Valentine's Day cards I had to trash them or put them away. To hold on to those things or keep them in plain view can only hurt. They only serve as constant reminders of better times. You must give your former relationships a proper burial to fully embrace a new relationship.

We are creatures of habit. When a relationship ends, we often feel lost. We were used to getting that late night phone call and being on the phone for hours. We were accustomed to having someone to do special things for during Valentine's Day, or maybe our birthday. We spent a lot of time in our partner's company. We knew what time they went to work and most times when they went to bed. Maybe he called at a certain time of day every day.

Now those calls have stopped. What you had become accustomed to is no longer there. You want to call and though you tell yourself over and over not to call. You find yourself picking up the phone and dialing the number. Your heart beats rapidly and the phone begins to ring. The anxiety you feel becomes so great you hurriedly hang up the phone, cry or beat yourself up for being so weak. You may find yourself frequenting one of his favorite places in hopes to run into him. The problem with this behavior is you weren't expecting to see him with someone else. Getting over someone that you love who is not good for you is never easy. However, you need to become self-disciplined with your behavior. Control your urges to contact, see or asking your girlfriends or his friends if they've seen him. These are just subtle ways of staying attached. Let it go. If he tells you he doesn't deserve you, believe Him and let him go.

> *Getting over someone that you love who is not good for you is never easy.*
>
> *You are in the process of recovery (uncovering the true you) and you don't want to reopen wounds of the past.*

You need to find new habits to replace the old ones. If you were used to going to a particular restaurant find a different one to go to. I'm not saying you couldn't ever go back. What I am saying is those places of familiarity, those places that you went to as a couple; they should be avoided during your healing period. You are in the process of recovery (uncovering the true you) and you don't want to reopen wounds of the past.

For a long time it was so hard for me to go anywhere because we did so many things together. A pool hall, a basketball court, and a restaurant even the beach had to be off limits. I would literally turn my head and focus on something pleasant in my mind when I passed places where we did things together. It wasn't always easy. Thing was, I had grown tired of being like a walking zombie. I wanted my life back. I wanted to be happy again. I wanted to smile again. I knew that the only way I could get there was to discipline myself. I had to think of the relationship breakup for what it was. I had to accept the fact that it was over. My sister coined it best when she described it as being "kicked in the stomach."

If you've ever been kicked or punched in the stomach, you know that is definitely not a good feeling. Imagine getting kicked or punched over and over and over. At some point we should realize it's just not worth it. As the old cliché says to continue to do the same thing the same way with the expectation of getting a different result is the definition of insanity.

No one can determine how long your process of healing will take, but what I can assure you is that if you are willing to move forward, help is available. If you are willing to rid yourself of toxic relationships, healthy ones are just on the horizon.

Our Time Will Come

It's never easy losing someone you love. It never feels good when you've invested time, energy and heart into a relationship only for someone to walk out of your life. It's even harder when they can walk out with no real explanation other than; they just no longer wanted to be there. Whether they give an explanation or not for ending the relationship, it is more important for you to focus on forward progress rather than painful reflection.

Speaking from experience, absolutely nothing feels good about being disappointed and getting your heart broken. One thing I have concluded through my experience of stress related health issues was that I was worth saving. My emotional, mental and physical wellbeing was more important than trying to keep someone in my life that no longer wanted to be there. So what do you do when loving him is killing you? You let Him go. I received another email when I was going through my situation which was such a blessing to me. Accredited to well-known leader, Bishop T.D. Jakes, this sums it up:

> **It is more important for you to focus on forward progress rather than painful reflection.**

Just because no one has been fortunate enough to realize what a gold mine you are, doesn't mean you shine any less.
Just because no one has been smart enough to figure out that you can't be topped, doesn't mean you stop being your best.
Just because no one has come along to share your life, doesn't give you permission to stop running.
Just because no one has realized how much of an awesome woman you are, doesn't mean they can affect your femininity.
Just because no one has shown up who can love you on your level, doesn't mean you have to sink to theirs.
Just because you deserve the very best there is, doesn't mean that life is always fair.

Just because God is still preparing your king, doesn't mean you are not a queen.
Just because your situation doesn't seem to be progressing right now, doesn't mean you need to change a thing.
Keep shining, keep running, keep hoping and keep praying, keep being exactly what and who you are already: complete.

> We can love so hard that we lose focus on the fact that we deserve better.

We can love so hard that we lose focus on the fact that we deserve better. We deserve to be in healthy, loving relationships. You don't have to settle. If someone is not treating you with the dignity and respect you deserve, let them go. You may feel like if you do your world will come to an end, but Baby I'm here to tell you, it won't!

Being raped of your love, ripped of your dignity and self-esteem is what you don't deserve. We need to let go of people who do not have our best interest at heart, and we need to do it seasonally. We make life-altering changes for the sake of keeping someone in our lives. We've got to come to a point that we love ourselves enough that we don't settle for substandard, counterfeit love. We've got to learn to listen to that inner voice and stop ignoring the signs. What do you want to be remembered for? Loving you or loving what killed you?

I'm not saying we should be paranoid. What I am saying is we need to stop making excuses. We many times blame ourselves. We say, if I had just done this differently or if I hadn't done that, things would be different. Honey, it is what it is. Let him go.

> We've got to come to a point that we love ourselves enough that we don't settle for substandard, counterfeit love. We've got to learn to listen to that inner voice and stop ignoring the signs. What do you want to be remembered for? Loving you or loving what killed you?

There will come a time when you will meet a man that will appreciate you for the rose, the incomparable and flawless gem that you are. Why settle for less than what you deserve? Why confront the "other woman" while he sits back and watches the two of you clamor over him? Why date a married man, knowing that nothing good can come from it? Why ride around late at night scoping him out with private detectives when you could be relaxing in bed at ease with yourself? When you settle for less, you hand over your power to someone who is undeserving of you, selfish, vain, and simply not into you or the relationship.

One thing I have come to understand is that adults are skilled. I don't care how you try to "clock" your man; if he wants to do something, he *will* find a way. As one movie aptly titled it, "It's a Guy Thing". No matter how wrong he is in a relationship, there are some men who will cover for other men simply because they *are* men. When a popular singer was in the news for dating violence, there were still men who stood by him and condoned his behavior. There is absolutely nothing you can do to stop your partner and you need to understand that. Everyone has been given free will.

The man for you is just waiting for you to unclog your drain. That man who is standing in the way needs to move. All the talking, crying, begging and making yourself sick can't make a person stay who doesn't want to be there. You cannot receive what is truly meant for you if you are holding on to something that is not yours to have. Let him go. Letting go of someone who continually shows you that they don't love you will be one of the best things you could do for yourself. Why make room for someone who has emotionally packed up and left the building? We struggle with the memory of the love we once had and the emotional connection that came with it. We need to let go of those memories so that we can move on to building healthier relationships.

> No matter how wrong he is in a relationship, there are some men who will cover for other men simply because they are men.

⚑ Red Flags

Before You Cross The Finish Line:

Many women know most times than not when something is wrong either during the beginning stages of the relationship or shortly thereafter. In a previous relationship I noticed that on occasions when I and my date went out he would walk a distance in front of me. Now I knew in my heart that there was something quite odd about that behavior.

As simple as that may sound, his body language and behavior had already told me that this guy was not comfortable being out in the public with me. I tried to make excuses for the behavior and soon talked myself out of what I knew in my heart. Though it still rested in the back of my mind, I continued on like it was nothing until he finally said he wasn't ready to be in a relationship.

Whatever our reason, we tend to talk ourselves out of what we know to be the truth. We try to rationalize odd behaviors in our minds in an effort to explain them away. We don't want to face the realities that the person we are attracted to is not attracted to us. Sadly enough, no doubt our family and friends have tried to tell us that the person we are choosing is not the one. They may look great *with* us, but they are not good *for* us. Ultimately it is our choice. In spite of it all there are those women that regardless of how badly they are treated, they will stay in the relationship to try to prove family members or friends wrong.

So what do we need to look out for that could potentially keep us out of unhealthy relationships? Let's examine some of the "red flags" Try not to rationalize and make excuses because in the end you are the one who will win.

Is he hard to reach on the weekends?

Unless he works in a maximum security prison or some other job that requires him to not be able to use a phone, you should be able to contact him. This could very well mean he could be spending that time with someone else.

Does he bad mouth his Ex-wife or former Girlfriends?

This has been something I have always questioned in my mind. In the early stages of dating a guy, I learned he had been married three times. He always blamed the Ex-wives as the reason for the marriages ending. He never took ownership of his part in the demise of his marriages. There is a saying that goes, "There are three sides to a story--your side, their side and the truth." Though I tried to make excuses, in the back of my mind his explanation always gnawed at me. Ultimately I found out he wasn't all he presented himself to be. So if a man doesn't take ownership he is probably not worth your time.

Given sufficient time. has he introduced you to his friends?

A man who is truly interested in you will at some point in the relationship want to introduce you to his friends. He won't treat you like some well kept secret. If a man doesn't introduce you to his friends, you need to reevaluate your position in the scheme of things. When a man is truly interested, he shows it.

Does he want to move to physical intimacy without any emotional attachment?

If a man tries to rush you into a relationship you need to not allow him to push you any faster than you feel you are ready to go. I remember a situation in which the guy tried extremely hard to get me to cave in and be in a relationship with him. I was just out of a relationship and thought it not in our best interest at that time to be involved on an intimate level. Although we enjoyed each other's company, he pushed to take it to the next level. Only when I was about to "cave in" did I find out another woman was expecting a child from him. I finally concluded that he was needy. He had to have someone in his life. Not the best way to go about it, but I guess it worked for him. Nevertheless, when a man pushes, it is my belief that there is some insecurity at work and we know insecurities are not good for a relationship no matter who is displaying the behavior.

Is He Rebounding?

A guy once told me whenever he broke up with a woman; he would quickly get involved with someone else to get over the pain of the break-up quicker. Now what do you think is going to happen once he is over the pain of that break-up? The likelihood of him breaking up with you is greater because his purpose for getting involved with you was wrong from the start. Men, just like women, need time to heal. You could very well end up getting your heart broken because he was only using you to fill a void.

Real Women, Real Talk

I had the opportunity to speak with several women who were willing to share their stories with me. I asked what they did once their relationship started going bad. I wanted these women to share their stories. Hopefully those of you who are facing this situation will benefit from these real life stories. You will see that you are not in this alone. These women realized they were in unhealthy relationships and found their way out. Though they took different paths, they all came to the realization that they were worth more than what someone else had valued them to be.

One of the young ladies had been out of a relationship for several years. She was excited and willing to share her story. As she began to write, she realized she had not dealt with the pain of her past. This is why it is so important to get help, to talk to someone. Get help from your pastor, priest or other professional counselor. It is so important that you can heal from your brokenness and the pain of the past.

Real Talk

I was involved in a relationship once and I thought the world of this person. I knew the relationship wasn't going anywhere but I stayed because I thought I could CHANGE him. I was cheated on, disrespected, abused, lied to, played and he stole from me. I lost friends over this guy because the people I confided in talked behind my back about what I was going through. When I woke up and realized I could not change him and that I wasn't the one breaking up our relationship I quit trying to change him and I changed. I got rid of all the negative people in my life whether it was female or male. I now surround myself with people that only want the best for me and people I can trust.

-Tiffany, Jacksonville, Fl

My son's father! I went to bat for him time and time again. I even busted another female's window out with my fist when I should have busted his. I lost 57 pounds stressing worrying and crying. The deciding factor that made me back off was because for every tear I shed for every pound I lost, he slept and ate well. Also, I figured out that he always came back to me. He was jobless and broke and almost 30. He needed me more than I need him. Its not fun going to work looking tore up and people always asking you what is wrong. If you sit and think about it, it's not worth it. Love isn't supposed to hurt unless you give an organ to that person to keep them alive. I still have mad love for him. I just won't do the same thing for him.
- Tonya, Jacksonville, Fl

Many of us can relate to these two women. We thought we could change them. They were abusive, they lied and were disrespectful. You perhaps did drive-bys and argued with "the other woman". You lost sleep, weight, money, days from work and cried yourself to sleep. I don't care how much someone talks to you about your situation only you can make the choice to stay or leave. You have got to decide that you are worth more mentally, physically, emotionally, spiritually and psychologically. You deserve to be treated like the beautiful, smart, vivacious and talented woman that you are.

Determine if you are struggling with self-esteem issues. This is normal if you have been dealing with situations like these described in this book. My hope is that you will experience a new normal. That love, joy, peace, and hope will fill your relationships and that this will not be a strange phenomenon, but an everyday expectation.

Until you decide to deal with negative self-esteem issues, you will have a hard time attracting those with good self-esteem. It is more important at this stage to have a healthy self-image than it is to be in a relationship.

Shortly after dealing with infidelity in my marriage, I sought out materials to help increase my self-esteem. I came across a book entitled; "How to Raise Your Self-Esteem" by Nathaniel Braden. And "Back from Betrayal", by Jennifer P. Schneider, M.D.

These books played a part in my saving grace. They touched on so many of the issues that I was dealing with at the time. I found myself practicing in the mirror and telling myself I was somebody. Now some of you will probably say, "I'm not standing in the mirror talking to myself." Amazingly enough it does help in solidifying your view of who you are and your self-worth; There is power in declaring and affirming yourself. Any time you are having difficulty breaking from a bad relationship, seek out the help that you need. There is no shame in securing professional help. You must free yourself and free those around you to seek out the help you or they need to be free mentally, physically, and emotionally, from imprisonment or oppression of any kind.

When I Know Better...I Me

When healing from a broken relationship, it is good to find avenues that will help in the healing process. Listed below are some things you can do during your recovery and transition from hopeless to wholeness.

♡ Take time out for yourself.

Find something you like to do and do it. It really is okay. Focus on relaxing, regrouping rethinking and resetting your priorities. Relax and take a few minutes for yourself. Reflect on things that are pleasant, good and pure. I've found that emptying my mind and thinking on pleasant and beautiful things can relax you. Sit in a quiet place when possible and take deep breathes. I've found that this releases a lot of tension. Regroup yourself after a setback. Determine how you are going to tackle your situation that will have the greatest positive impact. Rethink the choices you have made to see if they are indeed good choices and lastly, reset your priorities. Start over, putting in perspective what is truly more important and how it fits in the scheme of things.

♡ Eat Healthier

Whenever you can afford it, go natural as much as possible; eat plenty of fruits and vegetables. Eating healthy foods is one of the greatest ways you can live healthy and combat developing a disease. Many people become emotional eaters instead of becoming promotional eaters. Eat what promotes good health and clear thinking.

Exercise

It's so important to your overall wellbeing. Physical activity can prevent many major illnesses. Studies show that regular exercise can:

- ❖ promote healthy blood sugar levels to prevent or control diabetes
- ❖ promote bone density to protect against osteoporosis
- ❖ reduce the overall risk of cancer
- ❖ increase levels of HDL or "good" cholesterol -reducing the risk of developing heart disease
- ❖ lower high blood pressure-reducing the risk of developing heart disease
- ❖ boost the immune system
- ❖ boost self-confidence and help prevent depression
- ❖ in combination with a balanced diet, it helps to maintain a healthy weight

Build a Support Group

It is so important that you build yourself a good support group. Let them know what your goals are and how they can play an effective part in your recovery. When necessary, seek professional counseling. If you are employed, check with your employer. Many companies have Life Management groups that can assist you in finding the best possible care. Remember, there is no shame in seeking professional help. The shame is in having the need and forgoing the help available.

Watch Some Comedy

I bought movies that would make me laugh. Love and romance was out of the question. Laughter can be wonderful therapy. It is definitely good for what ails you. Invest in some good movie comedies and laugh yourself to health. "A merry heart does good like a medicine, but a broken spirit dries the bones" -- Proverbs 17:22

Recovery Killers

While some of these do-nots are easier said than done, practice makes perfect. You have been, or are going through a difficult time. Don't be so hard on yourself if you fall back from time to time. Be positive, patient and most of all gentle with yourself.

Don't Dwell On The Past

It is just that, the past. Think instead about how good you're going to feel once you overcome your loss. Peace of mind and healing is your goal.

Don't Contact

This of course does not apply to those who have children together. Their health and well-being is important too. If the father is willing to be a part of their life in a healthy relationship don't by any means try to stop that. However, if you are not one of those women in that situation, try to make as less contact as possible. It's not to say that one day you won't be able to talk to them ever again. The less contact the better, that way you can get them out of your system faster.

Don't Grieve Too Long

We don't always experience the grief of loss just once. We're likely to relive our grief on an anniversary, a holiday, a birthday or other events that were memorable. On the other hand don't remain paralyzed by the anger and loss. Feel it and give yourself permission to move forward.

DON'T STOP LIVING

You have so much to offer someone and just because this one or maybe another one didn't work don't mean you should stop. There will be one that will succeed.

Real Love

Although the same method doesn't work for everyone, it is necessary for you to find the way that will work for you. If it means no contact, then do that. If it means moving, talking to family members or getting professional counseling do it. Nothing and no one is worth you continually jeopardizing your health and wellbeing. Real love behaves in ways that makes us feel protected and cared for. Real love wants to embrace you and tell you it's going to be okay, I've got your back. Real love will not strike you or threaten you. Real love won't "lie" to you. It won't "cheat" your heart of the love it deserves and it won't "steal" your dignity away. Instead real love will be truthful. It will support you and it will honor you, respect and protect your dignity. Real love can't help but do you right. More importantly, you need to know that when loving him is hurting you, you need to, let it go. Love yourself enough to not allow anyone to treat you any less than the phenomenal woman that you are.

Feel free to use the pages in the back of the book as a journal and duplicate them as you need them. Write down your feelings every day. This will help you during your transitioning period. If you have made the decision to seek professional help, you can share these feelings with our counselor. I found that in writing down my feelings on paper, helped me to put things into perspective. As you move forward you will be able to look back and see how much progress you have made.

Always remember you are worth saving. Enjoy you, do you, love life, and your relationships will get better as you grow better and get better at loving you. When loving him is killing you, let him go, so you can live! Good luck and many blessings!

Sources

BUPA's health information team, healthinfo@bupa.com, August 2007.

The Benefits of Meditation in Daily Life, Jennifer Riener, May 28, 2008

©2000 - 2008 MamasHealth.com™. All rights reserved

©1998-2007 Mayo Foundation for Medical Education and Research (MFMER)

According to Nancy D. O'Reilly, Psych. D, Clinical Psychologist and founder of the Women Speak Project, © 1999-2007

McEwen, B. S. 1998. *Protective and Damaging Effects of Stress Mediators.* New England J. Med. 338:171-179.

Demitrack M.A. Neuroendocrine Research Strategies in Chronic Fatigue Syndrome. In: Chronic Fatigue and Related Immune Deficiency Syndromes (Goodnick PJ, Klimas NG, eds), pp 45-66. American Psychiatric Press, Inc. 1996.

Horwitz, R.J. and Horwitz, S.M. Adherence to Treatment and Health Outcomes, Archives of Internal Medicine, 133 (1993) 1863-1868.

Redelmeler, D.A., Rozin, P. and Kahneman, D. Understanding Patients' Decisions Cognitive and Emotional Perspectives, Journal of the American Medical Association, 270 (1993) 72-76.

Selye, H. *The Stress of My Life: A Scientist's Memoirs.* Van Nostrand Reinhold, New York, 1974.
Nesse, R. and Williams, G.C. *Why We Get Sick: The New Science of Darwinian Medicine.* Times Books, New York, 1994.

Clayton, P.J. Bereavement and Depression. J. Clin. Psychiatry, 51 (1990) 34.

WebMD Medical Reference from Healthwise@ 1995-2007, Healthwise, Incorporated

Bureau of Justice Statistics Special Report, U.S. Dept. of Justice.

Stress Responses In Biology and Medicine Stress of Life in Molecules, Cells, Organisms, and Psychosocial Communities Volume 1113 published November 2007
Ann. N.Y. Acad. Sci. 1113: 350–364 (2007). doi: 10.1196/annals.1391.028
Copyright © 2007 by the New York Academy of Sciences

Information Please® Database, © 2007 Pearson Education, Inc. All rights reserved. http://www.infoplease.com/ipa/A0781755.html

"Risk factors for injury to women from domestic violence". Demetrios N. Kyriacou, Deirdre Anglin, Ellen Taliaferro, Susan Stone, Toni Tubb, Judith A. Linden, Robert Muelleman, Erik Barton, and Jess F. Kraus. *The New England Journal of Medicine* 341:1892-98. December 16, 1999.

Dr. David Smith, The annual conference of Physicians For A Violence Free Society (February 1997)

Journey to Wholeness

Day _____

Gem for the day

What I will not allow to rule this day

Today's focus:

Spiritually

Physically

Emotionally

Relationally

Sexually

Intellectually

My Personal Affirmation Today :

Journey to Wholeness

Day _____

**Gem for the day**

_____

What I will not allow to rule this day

_____

Today's focus:

Spiritually

Physically

Emotionally

Relationally

Sexually

Intellectually

My Personal Affirmation Today :

Journey to Wholeness

Day ____

Gem for the day

What I will not allow to rule this day

Today's focus:

Spiritually

Physically

Emotionally

Relationally

Sexually

Intellectually

My Personal Affirmation Today :

Journey to Wholeness

Day ____

**Gem for the day**

What I will not allow to rule this day

Today's focus:

   Spiritually

   Physically

   Emotionally

   Relationally

   Sexually

   Intellectually

  My Personal Affirmation Today:

Journey to Wholeness

Day _____

Gem for the day

_____

What I will not allow to rule this day

_____

Today's focus:

  Spiritually

  Physically

  Emotionally

  Relationally

  Sexually

  Intellectually

  My Personal Affirmation Today :

Journey to Wholeness

Day _____

Gem for the day

_____

What I will not allow to rule this day

_____

Today's focus:

Spiritually

Physically

Emotionally

Relationally

Sexually

Intellectually

My Personal Affirmation Today :

Journey to Wholeness

Day _____

Gem for the day

_____

What I will not allow to rule this day

_____

Today's focus:

    Spiritually

    Physically

    Emotionally

    Relationally

    Sexually

    Intellectually

My Personal Affirmation Today :

Journey to Wholeness

Day _____

Gem for the day

_____

What I will not allow to rule this day

_____

Today's focus:

Spiritually

Physically

Emotionally

Relationally

Sexually

Intellectually

My Personal Affirmation Today :

Journey to Wholeness

Day _____

Gem for the day

_____

What I will not allow to rule this day

_____

Today's focus:

    Spiritually

    Physically

    Emotionally

    Relationally

    Sexually

    Intellectually

  My Personal Affirmation Today :

Journey to Wholeness

Day ____

**Gem for the day**

What I will not allow to rule this day

Today's focus:

Spiritually

Physically

Emotionally

Relationally

Sexually

Intellectually

My Personal Affirmation Today :

Journey to Wholeness

Day _____

Gem for the day

What I will not allow to rule this day

Today's focus:

Spiritually

Physically

Emotionally

Relationally

Sexually

Intellectually

My Personal Affirmation Today :

Journey to Wholeness

Day _____

Gem for the day

What I will not allow to rule this day

Today's focus:

▢ **Spiritually**

▢ **Physically**

▢ **Emotionally**

▢ **Relationally**

▢ **Sexually**

▢ **Intellectually**

My Personal Affirmation Today

ABOUT THE AUTHOR

Goldia G. Felder believes that women are an intricate part of the family structure and her mission is to help heal one woman at a time. Goldia helps train inner city kids in the martial arts, and has served helping citizens with disabilities. She has also worked in the mental health field and has had the opportunity to see firsthand what happens to people when they give up on life. Goldia's life tremendously changed after she endured her own personal trials and found the courage and strength to walk away. Her goal is to inform women on the hazards of unhealthy relationships, affirm their self-worth and help them to live the life they deserve. Goldia, who lives in Florida, is an alumnus of Bethune Cookman College and Edward Waters College in Jacksonville.